GUIDE TO
PORTO

Photographs: Stills, João Melo and
FISA Escudo de Oro photographic archives.

Text, layout and reproduction entirely conceived
and realised by the technical teams of
EDITORIAL FISA ESCUDO DE ORO, S.A.

Distribution: PRITI - Souvenirs, lda.
Tel. +351 96 4049468 - priti.souvenirs@gmail.com

⛉ ESCUDO DE ORO

INTRODUCTION

THE VISIT TO PORTO

Full of light and charm, cultured and enterprising, opened and generous, Porto possesses the special charm that characterises cities whose history spans thousands of years. Ancient Porto, the city that has lost count of the years and lived surrounded by walls for long periods of time, is the part we see from the other side of the river.

The historic quarter, catalogued as World Heritage in 1996, is where the dwellings are packed together and where you will find perched the streets of the Ribeira, Barredo and Miragaia neighbourhoods. On the outskirts of the once fortified perimeter is the part of the city that grew spectacularly in the 17th century as a consequence of the economic wealth generated by

Overall view of Porto from Vila Nova de Gaia.

the sale of its famous Porto wines. Further off, in the Foz do Douro neighbourhood at the mouth of the river, we find the part of Porto that overlooks the Atlantic Ocean from its beautiful promenades and such impressive fortresses as the Castelo do Queijo. Between Foz do Douro and the city centre are

The Castle of Queijo.

several peaceful neighbourhoods and parks that are also centres of culture.

To move around the city, the old trams, still operating, are the most attractive means of transport. There are only three lines left today, basically covering the city centre. However, the Metro is faster, taking travellers as far as the airport and further north to Póvoa de Varzim. The Dos Guindais funicular railway is the most practical way of getting between the upper part of Porto and La Ribeira neighbourhood. The Porto

Typical houses in Porto.

Night-time view.

Card gives users unlimited access to all public transport systems in the city, as well as to gain free admission to its main museums and discounts at other tourist attractions. The card is sold at tourist information offices and at the airport.

HISTORICAL BACKGROUND

Porto began its journey through history in the 7th century BC, when the first urban nucleus was built. This was later extended by the Romans, who established an important enclave in this area, from where they supervised the route that communicated with Lisbon and Braga. On one bank of the river was Cale, now Vila Nova de Gaia, and on the other, Portus, the Porto of today. Over the years, the city became established as the capital of the area then called County of Portucale, a name born from the fusion of ancient Portus and Cale.

This county, which until the year 1143 was attached to the Kingdom of León, was to become the seed of the future Portugal, a kingdom that would find its first monarch in the figure of Alfonso Henriques.

Between the 13th and 15th centuries, Porto engaged in intensive commercial and seafaring activities with such ports as those of Barcelona, Valencia, London and Antwerp. During those years, together with those of Vila Nova de Gaia, the city's dockyards were considered the most important in the country.

The closing years of the 16th century saw the beginning of a phase of great urban and administrative development. Little by little, the foundations for what would be one of the golden ages in the city's history were laid. This great period occurred in the 18th century. In the area of economy, the commerce of Porto wines reaped rich benefits. For decades, the Treaty

Avenida dos Aliados.

of Methuen (1703) signed with the English, guaranteed a solid source of revenue. In the artistic area, this was the great century of the baroque, which would change the physiognomy of the city forever. A key figure in this period was the Italian architect Nicolau Nasoni, the creator of many of the buildings greatly admired by visitors to Porto.

Traditionally a liberal and progressive city, between 1832 and 1833 the inhabitants of Porto fought against the absolutists who tried to take control. In recognition of Porto's heroic resistance and unbreakable adhesion to the Constitutional Charter, King Pedro IV gave the city the title of "Very noble, unconquered and always loyal".

In the early-20th century, the establishment of the Republic of Portugal brought the winds of change to Porto. This spirit of renovation materialised in the construction of the Avenue dos Aliados, representing

the start of a new era. More recently, while sharing the status of cultural capital of Europe with the Dutch city of Rotterdam in the year 2001, Porto embarked on another new age, one filled with dreams and projects. Today, the city has a population of 237,560, whilst Porto Metropolitan Area counts 1,816,045 inhabitants (2011 figures). This Metropolitan Area stretches as far as Póvoa de Varzim to the north, Oliveira de Azeméis to the south and Arouca to the east.

GASTRONOMY

The most typical dish in the city is traditional old *tripas à moda do Porto*. In the early-15th century, Portuguese ports witnessed a constant flow of men and boats going to sea in search of new conquests. The numerous expeditions of that period caused many expenses, which the State often could not afford. On such occasions, the government asked

Typical shops.

for the voluntary or involuntary collaboration of its citizens. So the inhabitants of Porto often had to give the meat of their livestock to the royal navy. All they had left were the

Delicious tripas à moda do Porto.

innards of the animals. For that reason the people of Porto were called *tri-peiros* and *tripas à moda do Porto* is a speciality of the local cuisine. Many dishes in the cuisine of Porto are also made from codfish prepared in different ways. The popularity of this fish is due to the fact that, for centuries, it was easy

Bacalhau à Gomes de Sá.

to fish and abundant. To this we must add the simplicity of its conservation. Amongst the many recipes, two are especially famous: *bacalhau à Gomes de Sá* and *bacalhau à João do Buraco*. Another popular local dish nowadays is *francesinha*, a sandwich filled with meat and covered in cheese and *francesinha* sauce, made from tomatoes, beer and chilli pepper.

THE WINES OF PORTO

The history of Porto wines could well have started with the arrival of the Romans in these lands, who first introduced grape-growing all

The Quinta do Vadado vineyards, Douro.

over the area. With time these wines would acquire great prestige, and in the 14th century they were already exported to countries like England. However, to really speak about Porto wines, we must wait until the 17th century, when British merchants discovered, it is thought by chance, the production technique based in interrupting the process of fermentation by adding neutral brandy. From 1703 and until 1757, the signature of the Treaty of Methuen gave the English the monopoly of practically all the wine trade. For this reason, it is very frequent to hear that Porto wines are as much English as they are Portuguese, a theory reinforced when you read words like Vintage, Tawny, Crusted or Ruby on the labels. Some even say that its taste is more English than Portuguese. In spite of this, nobody can question

The Porto Wine Museum.

that Porto wines are a genuine product of Portugal. They are produced in the *Região Demarcada do Douro*, the first designation of origin in wine history, are kept in

Barrels on the typical "rabelo" boats.

Quinta do Vale Meão, Douro: "pipas" or barrels.

the wineries of Vila Nova de Gaia –until 1986 the cellars could only be in that locality– and only Porto companies can export them, this being an indispensable condition for obtaining of *Região Demarcada do Douro* label.

Porto wines may be white or red, aged in barrels or in bottles. The most commonly used grapes are, for red wine, the Portuguese *touriga nacional, tinta cão, tinta barroca, tinta roriz* and the French *touriga francesa*, while for the white wines, *malvasía fina, códega* and *malvasía rei* predominate.

Brought to the wineries of Vila Nova de Gaia the wine is put in *pipas*, large barrels with an average capacity of 550 litres, and brandy is added to fulfil the conditions required by the *Instituto do*

Vinho do Porto (IVP). Once the aging process is complete, Porto wine is ready for consumption. The most popular are Ruby, a fruity young red with a ruby colour, Tawny, aged a minimum of three year in barrels, LBV (Late Bottled Vintage), with its strong flavour and very dark colour and, particularly, Vintage, wines made from the finest grapes, with a ageing period between ten and fifteen years.

For many years, Porto wines were transported from the area of the vineyards to the wineries of Vila Nova in boats called **rabelos**. The *rabelo* is a boat from the Douro with a large oar used as a rudder and two smaller oars on either side. With time, they became larger in size and a sail was added. With the arrival of trains and lorries, the *rabelos* lost the privilege of being the only adequate means of transport for the barrels. The few boats you can see today operate as tourist attractions whilst paying tribute to those earlier times.

Typical "rabelo" boats still ply the waters of the River Douro.

Overall view. In the background, Arrábida bridge.

CRAFTS

The craftsmanship of Porto is closely associated with its wine culture, from the making of barrels and baskets for the grape harvest to tin-plated articles such as funnels and watering cans. Traditional blue-and-white glazed tiles (*azulejos*) are also a typical product from the Porto

region and from the northern part of the country in general, together with embroidery and ceramics, mainly from the area around Barcelos.

TRADITIONS

As for its folklore, Portugal is a land famous for *fado*, songs that express so much feeling that time seems to stand still as their melo-

A typical glazed tile.

dies sound. Although they come from Lisbon and Coimbra, you can also listen to them and enjoy them in Porto.

The most popular festivity is the Night of Saint John, from June 23 to 24. The celebrations begin with a typical sardine dinner. This is followed by a firework display at the Luís I bridge, whilst parties take place all over the city with dancing until dawn and bonfires that people jump over for, according to tradition, this purifies the soul.

Night-time view.

A "fado" singer (typical restaurant O Fado, 16, Largo São João Novo).

1. THE OLD TOWN

We begin our visit to Porto in **Ribeira**, the oldest and best-known neighbourhood in the city. Ribeira is an area of daring colours, bustling taverns and fine restaurants. And also of clothes hanging in the sun, of golden reflections floating on the waters of the Douro and of renovations, more or less opportune, throughout its many years of history.

The remodelling that changed its physiognomy forever took place in the 17th century. Most of the walls protecting the city were demolished, the River Vila was buried underground and the main centre of commercial activities in Porto for centuries, **Praça da Ribeira** square was extended. John Whitehead, consul of Great Britain and a

Praça da Ribeira.

very knowledgeable man as regards architecture, was entrusted with the new design of the square. In spite of some later changes that did not respect the spirit of Whitehead's proposals, many think it still preserves a certain English style. The fountain that has presided over the square since the end of the 20th century has not escaped controversy regarding its sculpture, the work of the Portuguese sculptor José Rodrigues and known as the "Cubo da Ribeira". The arguments range from merely aesthetic issues to the adequacy of the space it occupies.

Another attraction in La Ribeira is the **Cais**, or dock, lined with small stalls in a multicolour display filled with attractive images. Looking

Cais da Ribeira.

out onto the river, it is easy to find *rabelos*, boats that for centuries have tirelessly transported Porto wine from the region of the Douro to the wine cellars of Vila Nova de Gaia. On this dock, we can admire the **Postigo do Carvão**, the only remaining gate of the eighteen originally built into the **Muralha Fernandina** walls (14th century). Beside Luís I bridge, moreover, is an interesting bronze **bas-relief** made

Luís I bridge.

The Postigo do Carvão gate.

by sculptor Teixeira Lopes in 1897 in honour of the victims of the *Ponte das Barcas* disaster. This tragedy took place on March 29th 1809, when French troops were about to seize the town. Many of the local inhab-

Bas-relief beside the Luís I bridge.

itants tried to escape by crossing the Douro on an improvised bridge made with boats, the so-called *Ponte das Barcas*. The precarious structure could not withstand so much weight, and it sank, causing the death of a great number of people.

Luís I bridge, which rises over the dock, is the best-known and most-photographed bridge in Porto. It was

Maria Pia bridge; in the background, São João bridge.

built according to plans drawn up by the Belgian engineer Théophile Seyrig, a follower of the famous Gustave Eiffel, and was inaugurated in 1886. It consists of two levels,

Entrance pillars from the former Pênsil suspension bridge, beside the Luís I bridge.

the upper level 392 metres long and the lower level 174 metres in length, though the main feature is the vast iron arch. Chronicles of the time state that 3,000 tons of iron were necessary for its construction. Its design is similar to that of **Maria Pia bridge**, which stands further away, though it does not have a lower floor. Maria Pia bridge was also designed by Seyrig and, constructed in 1877, predates Luís I bridge. Built as a railway bridge it has been disused since the São João bridge opened in 1991. Beside Luís I bridge we can see the entrance pillars to what used to be the **Pênsil suspension bridge**. This opened in 1841 to replace the ill-fated *Ponte das Barcas*, and was dismantled in 1887 when the new Luís I bridge entered into service.

Nearby is the station for the **Guindais funicular railway**, which connects with Rua Augusto

The Guindais funicular railway.

Rosa. An earlier funicular railway entered into service in 1891 to take passengers over the 61-metre difference in altitude between the Ribeira dock and the Batalha neighbourhood, but this closed due to a serious accident. The present funicular railway, which opened in 2004, is formed by a modern cabin with viewing windows. Another way

The Lada elevator.

of reaching the upper area of the city is by the elevator known as the **Elevador da Lada**, or Elevador da Ribeira, whose entrance is at Ribeira dock. This elevator also commands magnificent views over the other side of the river and surrounding neighbourhood.

A tour of these old Porto streets reveals many interesting houses and churches. From Cais da Ribeira we enter Cais da Estiva, coming to Largo do Terreiro which, in turn leads into Rua Alfândega Velha, where we find an interesting house, the **Casa do Infante**. An artistic inscription on the façade informs us that in this building, which dates to the mid-14th century, the Infante Dom Henrique, also known as Henry the Navigator, was born in 1394. In spite of this statement, many historians not only question the veracity of this, but even whether the prince was actually born in Porto at all. However, there is no doubt that these strong walls housed, firstly, the Mint, and later, the city Customs House (Alfândega). Now converted into the Municipal Historical Archive, the building went through successive alterations throughout its history, although it still preserves much of its original beauty.

Casa do Infante.

This house is just a stone's throw from **Praça do Infante Dom Henrique**. In the centre of the square we observe the huge sculptural ensemble erected at the end of the 19th century to honour the memory of the famous Portuguese navigator.

Ferreira Borges market.

Praça do Infante Dom Henrique: right, the Ferreira Borges Market; left, the Stock Exchange (Palácio da Bolsa) and the Church of São Francisco.

Right behind the monument you will find the old **Ferreira Borges Market**, built in 1885. Now used as a cultural centre after extensive refurbishment, the building is an excellent example of the so-called "cast iron" architecture of Porto. On the other side of the square stand the Stock Exchange and the Church of São Francisco.

Stock Exchange: Arabic Chamber.

Church of São Francisco.

with gold engravings. This artistic process, executed in various phases between the 17th and 18th centuries with the participation of renowned artists from northern Portugal, is thought to have required more than 200 kg of gold dust. The result, overly decorated for some, of extraordinary beauty for others, will leave no one interested in art indifferent.

Finally, on the corner with Rua Alfândega Velha stands the **Church**

Church of São Nicolau.

The **Stock Exchange** (Palácio da Bolsa), former headquarters of the Commercial Association of Porto, is where the convent of the Franciscans stood until 1832, when it was destroyed by fire. The foundation stone was laid in 1842 and the site was inaugurated on 21 November 1891. This building, of austere and elegant lines, is an outstanding example of neo-classical art in the city. The most famous and beautiful room in the palace is the Arabic Chamber. It was built between 1862 and 1880, and it is believed the builder found his inspiration in the Alhambra of Granada.

Only the church remains from the afore-mentioned Franciscan convent. The Gothic **Church of São Francisco** has a nave and two aisles, and represents an impressive exercise in elaborate baroque ornamentation with its walls decorated

Casa do Despacho da Ordem Terceira de São Francisco.

of São Nicolau, a simple but beautiful construction that dates to 1672.

We can admire one of many works in Porto by Nicolau Nasoni in Rua do Infante Dom Henrique: the **Casa do Despacho da Ordem Terceira de São Francisco**. The most outstanding feature in this building, completed between 1746 and 1752, is the Sessions Chamber, with its artistic ceiling and walls decorated

Miragaia.

Museum of Transport and Communications.

by paintings. In the same street stands the **Feitoria Inglesa**, or "English Factory". Built in English Palladian style in 1790, this housed an English gentlemen's club and the meeting place for the British Association, an organisation devoted to the Porto wine trade. Even today, the building operates as a club, its members linked to the wine trade, though it is no longer necessary to be British to join. The outstanding features inside the building include the staircase, the ballroom and the monumental kitchen.

In the opposite direction, Rua do Infante Dom Henrique leads into Rua Nova da Alfândega and **Miragaia**, another neighbourhood of typical narrow streets, once the home of fishermen, dockworkers and shipyard workers. The most interesting monuments in Miragaia include the enormous "New Customs Building", or Alfândega Nova, which dates back to the mid-19th century and now houses the **Museum of Transport and Communication**, and the **Church of São Pedro de Miragaia**, founded in medieval times though since greatly altered over the centuries.

Retracing our steps to Largo do Colégio, we can visit the **Church of São Lourenço** or "dos Grilos". Founded by the Jesuits, the construction of this pioneer of baroque architecture in Portugal began in 1573. However, the façade would not be completed until the early-18th century, when the site was finally concluded. With the expulsion of the Company of Jesus from the country, decreed in 1759 by the Marquis of Pombal, the site came into the possession of the order of the Discalced Augustinians in 1780, and from that moment on, it was known as the "Church of Grilos" (Crickets). According to popular tradition, we can trace the origin of this name to

Church of São Lourenço: High Altar and side chapel.

the dark tones of the monks' clothes, very similar to the colour of crickets. The church features a remarkable Mannerist façade and, in its interior, a magnificent altarpiece dedicated to the Virgin of Purification. The site now houses a **Museum of Sacred Art**.

We are but a stone's throw from Porto Cathedral, or the Sé de Porto. The square in which the cathedral is located, as we see it today, dates back to the 1940s. This was when the ancient medieval labyrinth was replaced by an open space presided over by an artistic *pelourinho*, an old pillory used for hanging the convicted, since 1945. Adjoining the cathedral is the **Casa do**

The Episcopal Palace.

Fragment of the "pelourinho" in Praça da Catedral.

Porto Cathedral and the Chapter House.

Cabido, built between 1717 and 1722. The most outstanding element in the building is the Chapter Room, adorned by glazed tiles from the original period of construction. The square is also enhanced by the presence of the **Episcopal Palace**, a structure of remarkable and elegant proportions built during the first half of the 18th century.

Porto Cathedral: cloister.

Porto Cathedral: the High Altar.

Porto Cathedral is a fortress-like building whose origins go back to the 12th century. The major alterations carried out over the course of time transformed the original Romanesque church into a building more in harmony with the baroque taste. The main façade, the main altarpiece, with its sumptuous Solomonic columns, and the ornamental tiles of the Gothic cloister, built in the 14th century, are all from that period. The robust twin towers on either side of the cathedral entrance, and the rose window over it, constitute the principal features of Romanesque art. The austere interior, divided into a nave and two aisles, finds sharp contrast in the magnificence of the main altarpiece and the ornamental wealth of the chapels. Amongst these, the most remarkable is the Chapel of O Santíssimo Sacramento (of the Blessed Sacrament), with its splendid altar, adorned in silver, which dates to the 17th century.

In Calçada de Vandoma, another interesting building is the **Antiga Casa da Câmara**, built in 2002 on the site of the city's former town hall. The building is also known as the "House of the 24", as this was where 24 people representing the

Chapel of O Santíssimo Sacramento.

different trades in Porto used to meet. Beside it is an equestrian statue of **Vimara Peres**, who conquered the city from the Moors in 868 and

Equestrian statue of Vimara Peres, and the Antiga Casa da Câmara.

Guerra Junqueiro House-Museum.

was made first Count of Portucale that same year.

In Rua de Dom Hugo, we can visit the **Guerra Junqueiro House-Museum**. Built as the residence of a cathedral canon in the mid-18th century, apparently by the artist Nicolau Nasoni, the museum now houses a large collection of pieces gathered together by the poet Guerra Junqueiro (1850-1923) including, particularly, precious metalwork, furniture and tapestries.

Not far from the cathedral is the **Torre da Cidade** (Rua de Dom Pedro Pitões). This tower, which was reconstructed in 1941, originally formed part of the Fernandina fortifications. It has three storeys and its main feature is the pointed arch on the north side.

We now enter Largo 1º de Dezembro, which leads us to the Church of Santa Clara whilst, at the crossroads with Rua do Duque de Loulé, we can admire the largest-surviving stretch of the **Muralha Fernandina**. These walls were built between 1336 and 1376 to replace an earlier fortified defensive enclosure rendered useless by the constant urban growth of Porto. It is known by this name because works were concluded during the reign of King Ferdinand I.

The **Church of Santa Clara** forms part of the old convent bearing the same name, whose construction began in 1416. In the early-18th century, the precincts were enlarged due to the increasing number of nuns living there, and several alterations were also made to the church. Many say that

Torre da Cidade tower.

the Church of Santa Clara is one of the most beautiful in the city. It has a remarkable façade, which brilliantly combines elements from the Manueline (Portuguese late Gothic) and renaissance styles, whilst the interior is decorated with gilt carvings. The choir stalls and the luxurious Main Chapel are the two most outstanding elements.

Praça da Liberdade.

2. PRAÇA DA LIBERDADE AND ENVIRONS

Praça da Liberdade square is a crossroads where the old and the new city merge. It is presided over by the equestrian statue of King

Town Hall.

Pedro IV, a monument ten metres high produced by the Belgium sculptor Antoine Calmels between 1862 and 1866. **Avenida dos Aliados** starts to the north of the square, and is lined by elegant early-20th century buildings. The avenue is closed at the upper end by **City Hall**, built between 1920 and 1957, whose most outstanding feature is the 70-metre-high tower. Particularly interesting amongst the Art Nouveau buildings on this avenue are the **Café Guarany** and the former **Café Imperial** (now a McDonald's restaurant).

The rear of the City Hall looks onto Praça da Trindade, opposite the vast **Church of Trindade**, whose size makes it one of the most impressive in the city. The church was built in the early-19th century in neoclassical style.

The old Café Imperial.

Adjoining Praça da Liberdade stand the famous São Bento Station and the **Church of Os Congregados**. The latter, which dates to the early-18th century, is easily recognisable due to its front, which is decorated

Church da Trindade.

Church of Os Congregados.

São Bento Station.

with glazed tiles. The construction of **São Bento Station** began in 1900 on a site occupied since by 1895 the Monastery of São Bento de Avé-Maria, hence its name. Although there is no doubt about the architectural value of the station, the work of Marques da Silva, it is quite obvious that its main attraction resides in the marvellous tile decorations in the main hall. Attributed to Jorge Colaço in 1916, the scenes

São Bento Station: main hall.

represent different episodes in the history of Porto and Portugal.

Continuing along Rua de 31 de Janeiro, we come to **Casa Vicent**, a house with a lovely front built in 1915, before entering a bustling pedestrian street, **Rua de Santa Catarina**. This street is lined by shops and business, but also contains interesting historic buildings such as the **Café Majestic**, the oldest and most popular café in Porto. Walking through its glass door is like travelling through a time tunnel. Nothing seems to have changed since its distant inauguration right at the end of the 19th century. Also on Rua de 31 de Janeiro is the **Capela das Almas**, a tiny chapel whose exterior is also decorated with typical glazed tiles. In this case, the scenes, painted in 1929, represent different episodes from the lives of Saint Francis of Assisi and Saint Catherine. An anecdote regarding this decoration is that, consciously or not, the artist confuses

Casa Vicent.

images corresponding to Saint Catherine of Siena with others of Saint Catherine of Alexandria.

The Chapel of As Animas stands on the corner with Rua de Fernandes Tomás, where we also find the main

Rua de Santa Catarina: Café Majestic.

The Bolhão market.

entrance to the **Bolhão market**. Opened in 1914, this is a vast space with a somewhat decadent air. The market, with its many shops and stalls, particularly selling cod, has scarcely changed over the years, and it is now a unique sight.

In nearby Rua de Passos Manuel is the city's commercial athenaeum, or **Ateneu Comercial do Porto**. This is one of the oldest institutions in the city with more than a hundred years of history, which, together with other private associations, contributed to promoting culture in Porto. In addition to having one of the most important private libraries of the city, it preserves a remarkable collection of art works.

Ateneo Comercial de Porto: Congress Chamber.

In the strikingly beautiful conference room, lectures, literary gatherings and book presentations take place. We find another classical local establishment in Rua de Costa Cabral, which we enter at the end of Rua de Santa Catarina. This is **A Pérola da Guiné** ("The Pearl of Guinea"), a shop specialising in the sale of coffee. In the same street is the **Fernando de Castro House-Museum**, formerly the residence of this merchant, poet,

caricaturist and, above all, collector, who died in 1946. The rooms in this house are decorated with lavish baroque ornamentation and artworks from the 16th to the 20th century.

At the opposite end of Rua de Santa Catarina, **Praça da Batalha** square also offers several points of interest, both from the architectural and historical points of view. To start with, according to tradition, its name recalls the bitter battle between the

Praça da Batalha.

inhabitants of Porto and the troops of Almanzor that ended with the defeat of the former and the destruction of the city by the latter. In the early-20th century, between 1919 and 1927, the square witnessed two military uprisings. The **Post Office building**, which dates to the end of the 18th century, and the **National Theatre São João** are the most interesting buildings here. The latter was inaugurated in 1798 although it was completely destroyed by a fire in 1908, after which it was totally reconstructed.

Adjoining the square stands the **Church of Santo Ildefonso**. An external staircase provides access to this church, which was built between 1730 and 1737 to replace one that dated back to medieval times. The tile work in the exterior is by Jorge Colaço, the same artist who created those at the São Bento station. In the interior you will find a high altarpiece built in 1745 by Miguel Francisco da Silva according to plans drawn up by the great master Nicolau Nasoni. The single nave is quite modest, whilst the polygonal ground plan is striking in its originality.

We now return to Praça da Liberdade to visit the **Church and Tower of Os Clérigos**, in nearby Rua dos Clérigos. This architectural complex, by Nicolau Nasoni, is one of the prime

Church of Santo Ildefonso.

Church of Os Clérigos.

this great master pursued most of his activities in the fields of painting and architecture in the city of Porto. Invariably, his name appears related to practically all the buildings constructed and remodelled during

Torre dos Clérigos tower.

examples of baroque art in Porto. It was built between 1732 and 1763. The church, with a profusely decorated façade and elliptic ground plan, features a remarkable altarpiece made from polychrome marble. However, the authentic jewel of the edifice is the 76-metre-high tower, which commands the finest panoramic views over Porto and surrounding area. Visible from all parts of the city, for many years it was a reference for boats sailing on the Douro. The place of this emblematic monument was known as the "hill of the hanged men", because convicts were buried here.

In contrast to the church, the external part of the tower displays a less colourful style, following the tendency of its creator in the latest years of his life. Nicolau Nasoni (1691-1773) is one of the major figures in the history of art of Porto in the 17th century. Born in Italy,

Praça de Gomes Teixeira.

that time. His mortal remains rest in the Church of Os Clérigos.

The church stands near **Praça de Gomes Teixeira**, with its artistic Fountain of the Lions, which dates back to 1886, and where we also find the **University**. Founded in 1911, the University of Porto is the largest in the country today, as regards both number of students and number of faculties, which are distributed all over the city. The building in Praça de Gomes Teixeira – named after the first rector of the university – was the

The University building.

Church of O Carmo.

original seat. Built in the early-19th century, it originally housed the Royal Navy and Trade Academy of Porto. Today, the site is occupied by the Rectory and the Science and Natural History museums.

On one corner of the square stands the **Church of O Carmo**, built in the second half of the 18th century. The church is graced by a fine rococo façade in three sections and a side wall decorated by a magnificent glazed tile panel installed in 1912. No tour of this area is complete without a visit to the **Librería Lello e Irmão** bookshop at nearby 144, Rua dos Carmelitas. This establishment has hardly changed since it first opened its doors in 1906, the Gothic Revival exterior tastefully harmonising with the Art Nouveau interior, which features a lovely carved wood staircase. It comes as no surprise to learn that the store served as an inspiration for the first Harry Potter

film. Next, opposite the Torre dos Clérigos tower in Rua Estrada da Assunção, we come to the **Casa Oriental**, a famous old establishment that specialises in salt cod, spices, coffee and chocolate.

Nearby, the **João Chagas Garden** is the perfect spot for a well-earned rest. However, the site is better known as **Cordoaria**, alluding to the work of the cord-makers in the Miragaia neighbourhood. The gardens became popular amongst the Porto middle classes in the 19th century

The Lello e Irmão bookshop.

after they were redesigned by a German landscaper. Today, though the site has lost much of this glamour, it still conserves a certain charm thanks to its pond, venerable trees and many sculptures. The garden is flanked by three large buildings.

The first is the *Cadeia da Relação*, which once housed the courts and prison, and whose construction dates to 1765-1796. The site now houses the **Portuguese Centre for Photography**, installed here in 1997. The second is the **Palace**

Palace of Justice.

Hospital of Santo António.

of Justice, built in 1961. Finally, we come to the **Hospital of Santo António**, which dates to the 18th century and sports a façade 177 metres long formed by five sections of different composition: one with a triangular pediment; one with Ionic columns; the others with arches.

We end this route in nearby Rua de **São Bento da Vitória**, where we find the church of the same name. A baroque choir decorated with thirty paintings representing episodes from the life of Saint Benedict is the main point of interest of this church, which was built between the 16th and 17th centuries by Benedict monks. In addition to the magnificent decoration of the choir, placing it with full honours among the most beautiful in Portugal, the church also features superb altarpieces and organs, dating back to the 18th century.

The interested in the work of Nicolau Nasoni should visit the

Church of Misericórdia in Rua das Flores, as Nasoni carried out alterations on the site. Both the façade and the interior are considered amongst the most outstanding examples of baroque architecture in Porto.

Church of São Bento da Vitória.

Soares dos Reis National Museum.

3. OTHER POINTS OF INTEREST

At 56, Rua de Dom Manuel II is the **Soares dos Reis National Museum**, the most important museum in Porto. Located in the Palace dos Carrancas, a building from the 18th century where they say Wellington, the English general, spent a night during the time he was fighting against the troops of Napoleon. Its rooms take us on a long journey through Portuguese painting, sculpture and archaeology until the 19th century. The works on show also include French and Flemish painting, and the most outstanding works of the sculptor Soares dos Reis (1847-1889).

Just 200 metres west of the museum are the lovely gardens of the **Crystal Palace**. This building provides another example of the importance Porto acquired in the field of so-called "cast-iron architecture". Inaugurated in 1861, it was designed as the venue for industrial and agricultural trade fairs celebrated in the city. Four years later, it provided the setting for the International Exhibition. After falling into disuse, it was demolished in 1951 to be replaced by the new and more modern Cristal Palace, with its gigantic dome as its main feature.

The **Romantic Museum**, which lies to the west of the Crystal Palace, enables us to form a very clear idea of how the Portuguese bourgeoisie

Crystal Palace and gardens.

from the 19th century lived. It is a house from that period where Charles Albert, Duke of Piedmont and King of Sardinia, spent his last years while in exile after the invasion of the Austrian army. Some of the rooms, especially those in which the monarch lived in until his death in 1843, have been renovated with historical accuracy.

Opposite the museum, the **Solar do Vinho do Porto**, installed in an old country house, is the ideal place to taste all Porto wine varieties. Moreover, from its terrace garden, which commands views over the Douro and its mouth, we can enjoy one of the finest sunsets in the city.

To learn more about Porto's wines, we should visit the **Museu do Vinho do Porto** (45, Rua Monchique). Inaugurated in 2004, the museum is housed in an 18th-century building beside the river that originally served as a warehouse for the customs service. Its exhibits illustrate the importance of the trade in wine for the city, and how this activity has developed over time.

Also beside the Douro, housed in the former Massarelos power station (51, Alameda de Basílio Teles),

Tram Museum.

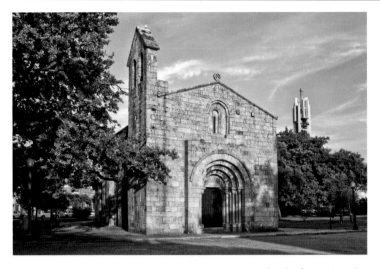

Church of São Martinho.

is the **Museu do Carro Eléctrico** or **Tram Museum**. Opened in 1992, this museum showcases a collection of trams, with the horse-drawn "American tram" as its most outstanding exhibit. The first mass form of transport in Porto, these trams first began to operate in the streets of the city on 15 May 1872. We must mention that Porto was the first city of Portugal to have a tram system.

To the north of the Crystal Palace gardens is **Cedofeita**, another of the city's historic old neighbourhoods, which grew up around the **Church of São Martinho** (Largo do Priorado). São Martinho is the oldest church in Porto and the only one built in Romanesque style. Some documents mention its existence as early as the year 1120. Extensive renovations carried out in the 16th and 17th century did not affect the basic Romanesque design, striking in its austerity. The main square in this neighbourhood is **Praça Mouzinho de**

Praça Mouzinho de Albuquerque.

Casa da Música.

Albuquerque, presided over by the Monument to the Peninsular War, which commemorates the victory of the British and Portuguese alliance over Napoleon's armies. This victory is symbolised at the top of the column by a lion straddling a dying eagle.

Beside the square is a building with an original structure: the **Casa da Música**, or House of Music, a symbol of innovative modern architecture in Porto. Its construction began in 1999 as part of the Porto 2001-European Capital of Culture Project, but the work suffered delays and was not completed until 2005. The site, which houses two concert halls, several rehearsals and recording rooms and a facility devoted to cyber music, was designed by the Dutch architect Rem Koolhaas, combines concrete with transparent glazed spaces. Guided tours are organised at the Casa da Música daily, at 11 am and 3 and 4.30 pm.

Also near Praça Mouzinho de Albuquerque, at 251, Rua Nossa Senhora de Fátima, is the **Marta Ortigão Sampaio House-Museum**. Here, we can admire naturalist painting from around the turn of the 20th century, mainly by Portuguese artists, as well as an interesting collection of jewellery from the late-17th to the 20th centuries.

The **Serralves Foundation**, in the Foz neighbourhood at 210, Rua de Serralves, is a cultural centre which houses the **Serralves House**, the **Museum of Contemporary Art**, a concert hall and 18 hectares of gardens. The oldest building here is the Serralves House, whose construction was commissioned by Carlos Alberto Cabral, second Count of Vizela, as a summer residence. Its construction began in 1925 and was completed

Serralves house and gardens.

only in 1944. Designed by the Porto architect Marques da Silva and this is the most outstanding Art Deco building in Portugal. In 1986, the State acquired both the house and its marvellous gardens. A foundation was established and the museum of contemporary art was installed in the Serralves House, a situation that continued until 1999 when the new building, designed by the architect Álvaro Siza, was inaugurated. With its straight lines and white walls, this new building has several levels, adapting to the terrain, whilst its large windows let in natural lighting that is rich in nuance. The concert hall, which is integrated into the site, opened in 2000. Finally, we come to the precious jewel that is the Serralves Garden, with its magnificent English- and

Serralves Foundation: two views of the Museum of Contemporary Art.

Rose garden in the Serralves gardens.

Dragão Stadium.

French-style gardens. Many are the visitors who go on tranquil strolls among its ponds, rosebushes, fountains and oak trees. More than just a cultural centre, the Serralves Foundation is a vast recreational area where you can admire some of the best contemporary art works, read under the shade of an apple tree or savour the specialities of its quaint Tea House.

Another interesting museum is the **Military Museum** (329, Rúa do Heroísmo), which boasts one of

the largest collections of miniature soldiers – around 16,000 – representing all the armies that have ever existed, with their historic development.

In Boavista neighbourhood is the **Bessa XXI Stadium**, home to Boavista FC, who play in the Portuguese Superliga. The stadium was completely refurbished for the 2004 Super Cup, as was the **Estádio do Dragão**, home of FC Porto, home to the city's most beloved football team, which is the Portuguese club with the most international trophies. The stadium is emblazoned with a figure of a dragon, emblem of the club, whilst the symbol of Boavista FC is a panther, as we are reminded by the sculpture of this animal at the entrance to the ground.

In Aldoar neighbourhood, close to the ocean now, we find Porto's great green "lung": the City Park, or **Parque da Cidade**. With an

Water Pavilion.

area of 83 hectares, 10 kilometres of paths and 4 ponds, the park is home to several species of aquatic birds. The outstanding architectural features here include the **Water Pavilion**, built for the 1998 Lisbon International Exposition. Designed by the architects Alexandre Burmester and José Carlos Gonçalves, the building creates the illusion of being suspended in mid-air. Beside the southeast entrance to the park stands the **Dr. António Cupertino de Miranda Foundation**, a cultural organisation that organises exhibitions and lectures. The foundation also runs the nearby **Museum of Paper Money**, which also features an unusual collection of more than 5,000 miniature cars.

Dr. António Cupertino de Miranda Foundation.

Foz do Douro beach.

Foz do Douro is the most westerly neighbourhood in Porto. Stretching between the mouth of the River and the Atlantic Ocean, this is one of the best-loved areas of the city due to its sea front promenade, lined with pavement cafés and lovely gardens. Particularly pleasant are the neat **Passeio Alegre gardens**, in which stands a fountain designed by Nasoni. Not far from here are the **Castle of São João Baptista**

Castle of São João Baptista.

Passeio Alegre.

and the old **São Miguel-o-Anjo lighthouse**, both of which date back to the 16th century. Continuing along the promenade, we reach the São Francisco Xavier Fortress, better known as **Castelo do Queijo** ("Cheese Castle"), as it was built on a rock shaped like a cheese. The castle, which dates to the 18th century, was built on the site of an earlier 15th-century fortress and is open to the public.

The São Miguel-o-Anjo lighthouse.

The Luis I bridge links Porto with Vila Nova de Gaia. In the heights, the Monastery of Serra do Pilar.

4. ENVIRONS OF PORTO

The city is surrounded by several townships that form part of what is known as Grande Porto (Greater Porto). These include some that are particularly interesting and are as old as the city itself, such as Vila Nova de Gaia and the coastal resorts of Matosinhos, Vila do Conde, Póvoa de Varzim and Espinho.

Monastery of Serra do Pilar.

VILA NOVA DE GAIA

Standing on the opposite bank of the River Douro, Vila Nova de Gaia is both Porto's neighbour and its old rival. In fact, its reconstruction towards the middle of the 13th century was the initiative of king Afonso III, who aimed at eroding the excessive power of the Bishopric of Porto. Throughout the 18th century, the popular cellars where the wines of Porto were conserved gave Vila Nova de Gaia extraordinary prosperity. The most outstanding monument in Vila Nova de Gaiais, which is somewhat smaller than Porto, is the Augustinian Monastery of Serra do Pilar. Its construction started in the 16th century although it was not completed until the first years of the 17th. An original church with circular ground plan and a

Renaissance cloister are two of its main points of interest. Its privileged setting also offers magnificent panoramic views of Porto. We reach Vila Nova de Gaia simply by crossing Luis I, whether on foot or by bus. The wineries, many of them open to the public, are found on the river bank. The best-known

The Calem winery.

Luis I bridge and Vila Nova de Gaia.

The wineries of Vila Nova de Gaia adjoin the river, for the wine was once transported by boat.

Aguda beach.

Aguda beach: aquarium.

are Ramos Pinto, Sandeman, Calem and Ferreira.
As for the beaches, those of Valadares, Aguda, Francelos, Lavadores and Miramar are amongst the

Miramar beach: Chapel of O Senhor da Pedra.

most popular with bathers in summer. At Miramar is the charming 18th-century Chapel of O Senhor da Pedra, whilst the attractions at Aguda include an aquarium and the Fishing Museum. Inland, near the river, is Gaia Biological Park, a 35-hectare agri-forest park that provides a habitat for hundreds

Gaia Biological Park.

Matosinhos: beach and sea front.

of animal species. Facilities at the park include information centre and such features as an old mill, now restored.

MATOSINHOS

Over the centuries, this town, with its long seafaring traditions, standing beside the Atlantic

Port of Matosinhos.

Church of O Bom Jesus, in Matosinhos.

Ocean near the mouth of the River Leça, has grown into the main fishing port in northern Portugal. With an important industrial and commercial system, Matosinhos also offers modern facilities for the celebration of competitions and congresses. The main monu-

Monastery of Leça do Bailio.

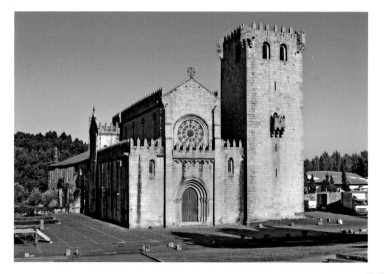

Partial view of Vila do Conde.

ment in the city is the Church of Bom Jesús, where the image of the "Senhor de Matosinhos" is worshipped. In this baroque church, built in the 18th century, the popular annual Whitsun pilgrimage takes place. Built in the 14th century, the Monastery of Leça do Bailio is rather older. Found in the village of the same name, this is an interesting example of a fortified church.

VILA DO CONDE

Located 30 kilometres north of Porto, Vila do Conde, a town with a privileged location at the mouth of the Ave river, lived the times of great the discoveries with great intensity. Many ships used by the Portuguese *conquistadors* in their expeditions were built at the dockyards here, which today are dedicated to the construction of fishing boats. In the past, its harbour also witnessed the arrival of many merchant ships bringing valuable cargos from Brazil. This prominence caused many skirmishes with pirate ships, against which its inhabitants fought with great determination from the Fort of São João Baptista, also known as Nossa Senhora da Assunção.

The most outstanding building here is the medieval Monastery of Santa Clara, reformed and

Vila do Conde boatyards.

Typical street in Vila do Conde.

extended during the 18th century. The façade of the church and part of the old cloister, both Gothic in style, have been preserved.

Of impressive dimensions, it was built on a hill on the site of a Celtic fort.

Water was transported to the mon-

Monastery of Santa Clara.

Vila do Conde: aqueduct.

Vila do Conde: parish church.

astery by an aqueduct, also from the 18th century, some fragments of which are still standing. The parish church (16th century) and handmade embroidery (there is a museum devoted to this craft) are just two of the main attractions in Vila do Conde.

PÓVOA DE VARZIM

Considered the heart of Costa Verde, or Green Coast, in the north of the country, Póvoa de Varzim is one of those towns where the arrival of summer brings an incredible increase in the number of inhabitants. It has a fantastic beach and many high-quality tourist facilities to welcome the thousands of visitors that flock here every year.

Among its most interesting monuments are the City Hall, its façade decorated with tile works, the baroque-style parish church and an old fort that stands sentry over this part of the coast. Worthy of special mention is the Municipal Museum of Ethnography and History, founded in 1937, which provides a broad vision of the evolution and customs of this coastal town.

ESPINHO

Twelve kilometres south of Porto, this old fishing village is, today,

Póvoa de Varzim: Town Hall.

a holiday resort with one of the oldest golf courses on the Iberian Peninsula. The club was founded by British citizens towards the end of the 19th century, when visitors looking for the therapeutic benefits of the sea and beaches began to come here. In addition to a spa offering thalassotherapy treatments, Espinho also has many hotels and a very popular casino.

Espinho beach.

CONTENTS

EDITORIAL FISA ESCUDO DE ORO, S.A.
Tel: +34 93 230 86 00
www.eoro.com

I.S.B.N. 978-84-378-2990-6
Printed in Spain
Legal Dep. B. 14869-2012